Want to see behind the scenes of how to design, build & launch your own high-converting book funnel? I've put together a special recording, previously reserved only for my private book funnel clients that deep dives into the entire Book Funnel Formula process and literally hands you the easy button to have all of this up and running in a matter of days.

If I'm still doing this by the time you are reading this book, then head straight over to your computer and watch the video now. It's absolutely free.

WATCH TODAY!

TheBookFunnelFormula.com/secret

THE BOOK FUNNEL FORMULA

7 STEPS TO TRANSFORM YOUR BOOK INTO AN ONLINE SELLING MACHINE

GARY WHITE

PUBLISHED BY BITE SIZED BOOKS

Copyright © 2020 by Gary White

All rights reserved. Without limiting the rights under copyright reserved above, no part of this book may be reproduced, stored or introduced into a retrieval system, or transmitted, in any form or by any means (electronic, mechanical, photocopying, recording or otherwise), without the prior written permission of both the copyright owner and the publisher.

ISBN: 978-1-7341187-9-7

110220

Bite Sized Books publishes short, helpful books or shooks™ for Main Street business owners to attract new customers. Shooks are easy-to-create, quick-to-read short books. They are designed to be read by prospective customers, clients or patients, in about an hour. Bite Sized Books offers a painless process to enable entrepreneurs and business owners to benefit from the authority that comes from being a published author, without the hassle and time commitment normally associated with writing a book. Do you have an idea for a bite sized book you would like us to publish? Visit BiteSizedBooks.com for more details.

To my amazing partner Sammi, for all her love, support, and for never doubting me on this unconventional journey.

PRAISE FOR
THE BOOK FUNNEL FORMULA

"We now use multiple book funnels to drive hundreds of highly qualified new customers into our business every single day. If you have the opportunity to work with or learn from Gary, I wholeheartedly recommend you follow his guidance to create your own high converting book funnel."

Brendan Kane
Bestselling Author & International Speaker
Strategist for Fortune 500 Corporations

Gary is handing you the strategies that I've paid him literally thousands of dollars to learn and implement! If you are launching a book to start or grow your business this is a must read for sure!"

Jordan Platten
Author, Speaker and Founder of Affluent.co

"Authoring and publishing a book is only half of the equation, and as I tell my publishing clients, it's frankly the easy part. The more challenging half is promoting, marketing and making money from your book (and I am not referring to the dollar or two you make when you sell a book). In this comprehensive A to Z guide, book launch and marketing expert, Gary White, peels back the curtain and reveals the exact steps and requirements to create an auto-pilot book funnel. *The Book Funnel Formula* is a book I recommend to my clients and anyone looking to fully leverage his or her book for maximum exposure and profits."

Mike Capuzzi
Publisher & Bestselling Author

"If you want a book funnel that converts, Gary is definitely your guy."

Brian Souza
New York Times Bestselling Author,
CEO & Founder of ProductivityDrivers

"Gary is the expert when it comes to designing, building and launching book funnels. This book is a top-notch guide to have the same formula up and running for your own book. If you have a powerful teaching, story or message to share with the world, Gary's book is your key to unlocking your success."

Andrew Gottlieb
Author, Founder of No Typical Moments

"This is a step-by-step playbook to not just get your book into the hands of your ideal readers, but actually turn those readers into high paying clients and customers. If you know your book has the ability to impact your audience as well as grow your business, then you must read *The Book Funnel Formula* Today."

Adam Markel
CEO, International Keynote Speaker
& #1 WSJ Bestselling Author

"As a Forbes Top 10 business coach who helps experts scale online coaching and consulting offers, I consistently find myself recommending The Book Funnel Formula to my clients and anyone looking to further leverage their expertise with (+ actually PROFIT from) their book. Inside Gary shares not just why authors NEED a book funnel to avoid being left behind but also, even more fascinatingly, the psychology behind converting readers into high paying clients and customers."

Lauren Tickner
Founder & CEO of Impact School,
Forbes Top 10 Business Coach

"I've personally worked with Gary on projects promoting book funnels he's created with ads. Without a doubt, Gary understands what it takes to generate not only readers, but profitable customers from a book funnel. Reading this will be vital to having a book funnel that makes money from advertising."

Jason Hornung
Founder of JH Media &
AcademyOfAdvertising.com

"Confession time! I have a "man-crush" on Gary! It happened rather fast following meeting him at a seminar several years ago. His knowledge and hands-on experience of funnels and more importantly how to turn them into customer getting, revenue-generating, profit-producing machines immediately got my attention. Whenever I need help and advice or I'm having problems with my book funnels, Gary is the person I call. My only worry is, he's now sharing these closely guarded secrets in this book and I was hoping to keep it all to myself! For anyone with a book, or quite frankly, any business owner wanting more customers, this is a must read!"

Dean Holland
Author, Speaker, Trainer
& CEO of InternetProfits

CONTENTS

Who Should Read This Book? 1
My Promise to You 7
Introduction 9

Part 1—Introducing the Book Funnel Formula
Chapter 1: The Truth About Books 17
Chapter 2: Paving the Yellow Brick Road 25
Chapter 3: Unlocking the Formula 29
Chapter 4: The Most Important Metric 39
Chapter 5: Activating Your Unlimited
Advertising Budget 43

Part 2—Book Funnel Building Blocks
Chapter 6: The 3 Core Phases 49
Chapter 7: Phase 1: Acquire 51
   Identify Interest 52
   Converting the Sale 56
Chapter 8: Phase 2: Liquidate 67
   The Closest Thing to Free Money 68
   Solving the Next Problem 72
   Squeezing the Orange 79
Chapter 9: Phase 3: Ascend 83
   The Bridge 84
   Monetization Loop 96

Part 3—Making It Happen!

Chapter 10: How I Help People Just Like You 111
Chapter 11: Your Next Step 115

About Gary White 119
Key Resources 121

WHO SHOULD READ THIS BOOK?

This is an intentionally short book with all fluff and filler removed, designed to be read in a single sitting so you can gain the insights as quickly and effectively as possible. I don't want to waste your time if it's not a good fit, so please take a few minutes and read this entire section to see if *The Book Funnel Formula* is a smart investment of your time, energy and focus.

First and foremost, it's important to make clear that *The Book Funnel Formula* is NOT for the next Stephen King or J. K. Rowling. By that I mean, the concepts revealed inside this book are not tried and tested nor ever intended to be used by fiction authors.

Instead, my focus is on helping influential leaders, authorities, experts and entrepreneurs transform their nonfiction books into powerful online customer-acquisition tools engineered to spread their message, grow their audience and exponentially increase their income.

Specifically, I created *The Book Funnel Formula* for two types of people:
1. The established thought leader with a proven track record of results and experience who authored a book to share their ideas and expertise.
2. The savvy business owner who recognized a book's ability to establish credibility and authority within their marketplace.

If you fall into one or both of the above categories, you will be happy to know I wrote this book for you and your specific situation, needs and opportunities.

After working with and running the marketing for many expert authors and influential business owners over the past couple of years, I have had the privilege to see behind the curtain and gain a unique insight into what works and what doesn't. Some see extraordinary levels of wealth and success, others get known but reap very little financial reward and many are never able to make the impact they feel they should.

I decided to write *The Book Funnel Formula* for three reasons:
1. To shift your focus from attempting to profit from merely your book itself to considering

your book as the filtration device that raises the metaphorical hand of your ideal audience and identifies your dream customers.
2. To share a far more profitable way of leveraging online advertising to predictably and consistently grow your reach, influence and credibility while customizing the entire customer journey so your readers are perfectly positioned to do additional business with you (where the real money is).
3. To invite you to utilize a new marketing approach that regains control of the sales process so you get paid to communicate directly with your readers, build rapport and offer greater value through additional products and services without the restrictions of mainstream publishers, online marketplaces and retailers.

Ultimately I want to pick up where most publishers or ghostwriters fall short because they don't care to create books with clear intentions and often have no idea what to do once the book is actually produced. This can leave authors feeling like marketing is some slimy activity that's hard, mysterious and only occupied by people with bad intentions.

But without good marketing, authors are often left stuck with a big ol' stack of physical copies gathering dust in the garage and no clarity on how to move forward. Now while that is disappointing for them, the greater scandal is for those who will miss out on the opportunity to read, learn and benefit from the information contained within those pages. If you believe that your book is valuable, I believe it is your duty to get it out to those that really need it.

Luckily, this book will provide a clear path for how to get your book into the hands of your ideal readers, identify them, nurture them and create desire within them so they are motivated to want more of your talents, experience and expertise.

The Book Funnel Formula Was Written for the Person Who Agrees With These Seven Beliefs:

1. Authoring a book is the most effective way to establish influence, credibility and authority within any marketplace.
2. A book is one of the best ways to communicate why your products or services will help others solve a problem or take advantage of a new opportunity.
3. The measure of a good book is the impact it has on the reader as well as its ability to drive a desired action.

4. The author should be in control of the book sales process and should be the one who ultimately benefits from it.
5. It is fundamental to know who purchased your book and to have a direct line of communication with them.
6. By following up with readers once they read your book, they are more likely to purchase your additional products and services.
7. Creating an email database of buyers is the most valuable asset you can create in your business.

If you believe a book on its own is rarely a truly profitable, high-impact business and you are not afraid to offer additional options for your reader to upgrade their experience and consume your content through an ecosystem of highly profitable, targeted products and services, then I wrote this book for you, so please keep reading.

"Coming from a traditional publishing deal on my first book where I had little control over sales and marketing, I knew there had to be a faster and more effective way to use my book to drive new leads and customers into my business which led me to working with Gary.

"Gary was able to break down and simplify the process of creating a book funnel that successfully converted cold visitors into customers from scratch, as well as show my team how to effectively position additional offers into the funnel to drive additional revenue from every book sale.

"Working with Gary has helped us discover the almost limitless potential that comes from being in full control of the sales process, so much so that I even decided to self-publish my second book (instead of accepting another publishing deal) so that I could retain complete control of the sales and marketing.

"We now use multiple book funnels to drive hundreds of highly qualified new customers into our business every single day. If you have the opportunity to work with or learn from Gary, I wholeheartedly recommend you follow his guidance to create your own high converting book funnel."

Brendan Kane—Bestselling Author, International Speaker, Business Innovation Strategist for Fortune 500 Corporations, Brands, and Celebrities

MY PROMISE TO YOU

It is my sincerest belief that the author should be in control of the book sales process and be able to communicate directly with their readers to offer them more value through additional products and services without the restrictions of mainstream publishers, online marketplaces and retailers.

My intention is to open your eyes to the possibilities of taking back control of the book sales process and motivate you to take action and get started creating your own book marketing machine so you can confidently and predictably spread your message, grow your audience and increase your income.

A book funnel, when executed correctly, will give you (as an author and business owner) a fully automated system that creates a predictable and consistent flow of new customers while also providing greater value to those customers by offering them additional opportunities to learn from your expertise through multiple mediums.

Ultimately, by implementing the methods outlined in this book, you will gain the ability to deliver a much higher quality customer experience to your reader while rapidly increasing your income so you can scale your marketing, exposure and reach to levels you previously may not have thought possible.

That is the promise of *The Book Funnel Formula*.

INTRODUCTION

It's no secret that publishing a book is the ultimate credibility tool for positioning yourself as the go-to expert within your respective industry. Having your name on the cover can increase your influence, differentiate you from your competition and enable you to grow an audience around your message, ideas and methodologies.

This isn't anything particularly new or even groundbreaking. It's been happening for hundreds of years. What adds greater depth to this concept though, is exponentially more powerful and yet far less recognized—**a book's unique ability to identify your potential dream customers.**

Regardless of industry or marketplace, there is no better potential customer than the one who is already predispositioned to who you are, what you stand for and how you are already uniquely qualified to help them. Not only does this make selling superfluous, it also organically manufactures a higher quality of customer who is likely to spend more and get better results.

A few years ago I heard from the founder of a software startup who was frustrated that although he knew his software had the ability to literally change people's lives for the better, the level of complexity and steep learning curve for utilizing it meant users often became frustrated and cancelled their account prior to experiencing significant success with it.

What he did next changed the way I look at both books and business forever. Instead of ploughing more of his dwindling resources into further developing and refining the user interface or sinking more cash into the payroll for additional customer support representatives, he decided to do something very different. He decided to write a book.

By using the book as a pre-frame to get people into the software, he was able to articulate the overarching strategies that were a prerequisite to achieving success using the software and install belief by showcasing both his own results and those of his most successful users. It was the equivalent of being able to provide a private consultation and personal pep talk to every potential new user to ensure they were set up for success from the very beginning.

Not only was he now able to identify his potential customers with his book, but he was also able to cultivate his dream customers on demand. His exposure grew, his software sales went up, and his customer support enquiries dropped significantly. But what was even more powerful was what he discovered next.

He was able to clearly identify from his Customer Relationship Management (CRM) system that new software users who had come into the business after getting the book were 5x more likely to stick with the software for more than 6 months than those who came in without and were, therefore, worth 5x more to the business.

Those were the users experiencing real success. He had found his dream customers. Note that he did not create the book as some vanity project to achieve bestseller status and gain recognition (which can happen as a by-product), but the book was written with clear intent for what it is to achieve.

This lesson can be applied far broader than just software. I have since seen and implemented the same process for everything from coaches, consultants and online memberships to done-for-you service businesses and even brick and mortar stores.

So why doesn't every business founder or owner have a book? After all, there are a multitude of "experts" teaching that you need to write a book and even how to write one quickly and most efficiently. Perhaps you have been through that process yourself? But the big gap is what comes next...

Most people who write and publish a book put all of their efforts into a big launch at the beginning to achieve a bestseller status (which can be beneficial but does not translate directly into income), and then their efforts simply begin to fizzle out over time due to a loss in momentum.

I call this the "book launch hangover." You may have experienced it if you have already traditionally "launched" your book. You ask your friends, family, colleagues and clients to purchase a copy to boost your initial sales, but it's almost impossible to keep that initial momentum going. And before you know it, your book is gathering dust on the digital bookshelf.

In the coming chapters, I will show you how *The Book Funnel Formula* will compound your efforts, meaning that your book sales will grow consistently and predictably over time.

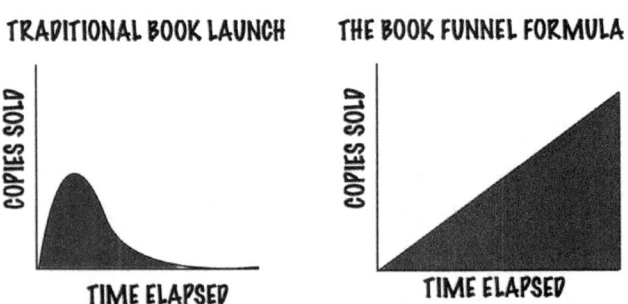

It's one thing to have a book. It's another to know what to do with it.

I wrote this book because I recognized that inevitably almost every nonfiction author runs into at least 1 of these 3 key problems:

1. I have a book, but no one knows about it.
2. My book is selling, but I've got no idea who bought it.
3. My ideal prospects have my book, but I can't get them to take the next step with me.

Do Any of the Above Statements Sound Familiar?

If so, keep reading because I'm about to show you exactly how *The Book Funnel Formula* solves each one of these problems by taking a completely different approach to marketing and selling your book—one that allows you to take back control and facilitate the entire sales process on your own terms.

You control the amount of visitors being exposed to your book, you collect and segment all of your customer data and you customize the entire customer journey. This cultivates readers that are perfectly positioned to do additional and future business with you, all while providing a much higher quality customer experience.

PART 1

INTRODUCING THE BOOK FUNNEL FORMULA

"Over the years I've worked with a number of so-called 'experts' in the funnel building business who failed to live up to expectations. After being referred to Gary through a colleague, I decided to work with him on the launch of my book. I could not be more pleased with his level of expertise, professionalism—and most importantly, results! If you want a book funnel that converts, Gary is definitely your guy."

Brian Souza—New York Times Bestselling Author, CEO & Founder of ProductivityDrivers

CHAPTER 1

THE TRUTH ABOUT BOOKS

Historically, getting a publishing deal was an essential part of becoming an author. It was almost pointless writing a book without a publishing deal in place because only publishing houses had the power and resources to print and distribute a large number of books. They held the keys to the kingdom.

While the past decade has seen the general consumption of books remain consistent, the barrier to entry for authoring a book has lowered considerably through a combination of developments in technology as well as the decentralization of information. This has caused the supply of books to explode, and there are now many more books than there are readers for those books.

There is a scary statistic for any author who is trying to stand out and capture audience attention.

95% of books sell less than 100 copies.
Ouch!

It's not that those books are necessarily bad; it's simply a supply and demand problem.

It means that publishing a book is no longer the goal; getting your book into the hands of your dream customers is, and for that you need eyeballs. *After all, if no one knows about your book, how do you expect to sell it?* The key ingredient to selling anything online is getting eyeballs on what you have to offer. This is known as "traffic."

Assuming you have created a book that solves a big problem for your desired audience, whether that be your dream consulting client, the perfect user for your software, the perfect business owner for your professional services or an ideal consumer of your recurring membership program, it's likely you're going to want to list it on "the world's largest bookstore" (Amazon.com).

But while Amazon has lots of traffic and lots of eyeballs, the downside is you have no control over that traffic. You might have 100 interested people view your book one day and absolutely zero the next. This inconsistency is a big problem in itself, but the even more daunting prospect is that you have absolutely no way of knowing.

I frequently see speakers give the call-to-action from stage at the end of their talk to go get their book on Amazon. While at first thought this seems like a great opportunity for exposure, but without a clear method to track results, it's impossible to know how many people in the audience: 1) took action to view the book, 2) actually purchased the book, 3) went on to result in future business.

This goes for all promotional activities, whether you are speaking from the stage, being interviewed on a podcast, recording a YouTube video or publishing a guest blog post. If you are directing that traffic to a third party like Amazon.com without direct access to the performance metrics, it's impossible to identify their effectiveness and evaluate whether to continue using them as a tool for growth or pivot and try something new. Only what is measured can be improved. This is why most people in this space fail to gain any real traction at all.

But there's a greater problem when directing potential buyers to a third party site like Amazon.com to purchase your book; it is Amazon acquiring the customer, not you. This is what makes them so powerful because they obtain the very commodity which in this day and age is more valuable than oil or gold: the customer data.

An email list of buyers is the most valuable asset you can create in your business because a buyer (by the very definition) buys stuff. And if they've shown interest already in what you offer and if they have had a good experience, it's likely at some point in the future they will buy from you again and again.

Some savvy authors embed call-to-actions within their books prompting readers to go visit their website, or better yet, receive bonus materials in return for entering their email address (like you'll see within the pages of this book), allowing them to start building a database of readers. However, these methods commonly produce extremely low conversion rates and don't provide a direct communication channel with the reader until after they have actually read the book (no good for the majority of book sales which get readers excited at the time of purchase then sit on the coffee table for six months).

You may think that Jeff Bezos is there to help you sell your book, but believe me, the scales are tipped far in his corporation's favor. They get traffic to their website for free (through your referral), and they happily take a cut for facilitating the sale on a product they didn't have to create. They also receive all of the buying data which provides a direct channel of ongoing communication with the customer for their future marketing efforts. AND they even have the audaciousness to say "People who purchased this, also purchased this..."

Amazon is a master at getting all of us to add additional items to our cart before checking out, and they're also masters at getting us all to continue buying by showing us other products we might like even after we think we're done shopping. *Why does Amazon do this?* Because it works.

Last year, this simple technique was responsible for 35% of Amazon's gross sales. That's $37 billion dollars! Amazon's total profit was $47 billion, which means that without this simple technique of offering other "add on" products, they would have generated only 22% of that profit.

Amazon profits by selling more additional items to YOUR customers without sharing any of that additional revenue with you. It's Amazon that now holds the keys to the kingdom.

When I explain this to potential clients and I witness the natural "aha" moment go off in their head, it's almost always met with the next statement: "Well I could sell my book on my website."

Selling your book straight from your website would be the logical next step to gain control of the selling process and begin acquiring the customer data to know who is actually purchasing your book.

In reality though, it's extremely difficult to make any real money by selling your book on your website. Firstly, you already need a source of traffic like a social media following or an existing email database to be able to let people know where to go to get the book. Once again, without eyeballs on the offer, no one is going to know where or how to purchase.

By being in control of the sales process, it is possible to begin your own online advertising that has visitors click on an ad for your book and head over to your website to find out more and potentially purchase from there. This is beneficial because you don't require the existing audience, and advertising creates a predictable source of traffic that you can control. *Sounds good so far, right?* But here's where this method falls short...

Typically it's going to cost anywhere from $10–$20 in advertising to sell one book on your website. The problem with that is the typical book on a website is only going to cost up to $19.95. So even if you're able to get your costs down, once you factor in the cost to print and ship the book, you can find yourself losing money on every single book you put out into the marketplace. That, of course, is not sustainable. And if you are spending more money than you make, it becomes very difficult to grow your audience and get your message out at scale.

But what if there was another way?

In contrast, what if you could take a leaf out of Amazon's book and offer your book buyers the opportunity to purchase additional items during the checkout process by guiding them through a sequence of predefined steps, which this time, you have full control over?

Better still, instead of Amazon offering other people's products to your book buyers and then not sharing the additional revenue, you begin presenting your book buyers with the opportunity to upgrade their orders to include your own additional products that complement the book while you keep 100% of the additional revenue so you can actually become profitable.

How much more reliable would your sales process be?

How much more impact could you deliver to your readers?

This is why we use *The Book Funnel Formula*.

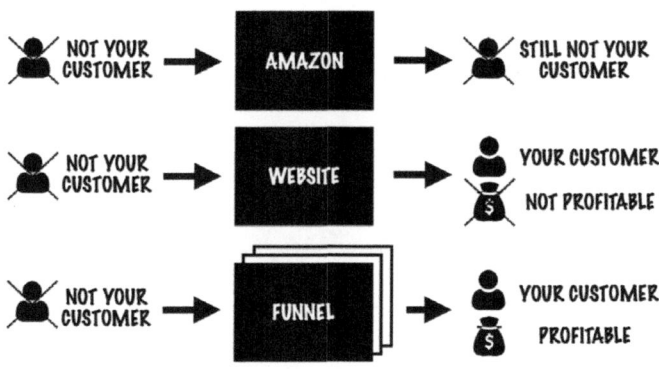

It's important not to worry if you don't yet have an arsenal of additional products that complement your book because creating them is much quicker and easier than you might think. We'll discuss exactly what type of additional products to create later in this book, and more importantly, exactly how to offer them so that you not only increase your income but your customers also receive a better experience and achieve greater results.

But before that, just like Dorothy and Toto, we need to take a trip to the Emerald City.

Ok, let me explain...

CHAPTER 2

PAVING THE YELLOW BRICK ROAD

"It's always best to start at the beginning—and all you do is follow the Yellow Brick Road."
—Glinda, the Good Witch of Oz

Everyone has an Oz, a calling, an outcome, a result they are trying to get to. You are reading this book, right now, because you want to spread your message, grow your audience and ultimately increase your income.

While your book is a fundamental piece of doing that and has the ability to change someone's life on its own, it is merely a roadmap for the overarching metaphorical "journey" towards the end result. Your book is the map that allows your reader to navigate the journey to Oz themselves. Many will get lost and give up along the way, some will persevere and require additional guidance, and others, they will just want to take an Uber.

It's important that you first identify what Oz is for your target reader because they are going to be your dream customer. If your book is about weight loss, their Oz might be feeling comfortable within their own body. If your book is about starting a business, their Oz might be financial freedom. If your book is about learning to play guitar, their Oz might be playing a live concert.

They are reading your book because they have a desire for a quantifiable end result (QER), and it's your responsibility to help guide them along their yellow brick road to reach Oz and achieve that desired outcome. I like to refer to this process as "The Success Path."

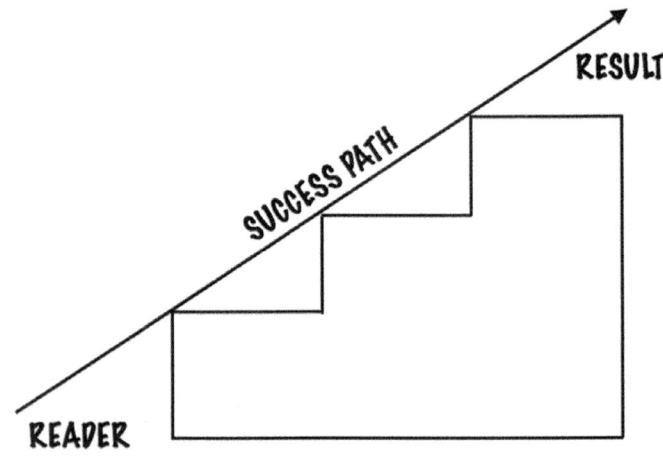

Once you establish what Oz looks like for your reader, you can begin to build out the elements to facilitate the journey. Different readers will require and have the means to pay you for different levels of facilitation. The measure of an ideal customer is that they are both willing and able to pay for your assistance.

Many will want to learn more from afar, but those who opted to take the Uber will prefer the fast-track route and will want to work with you directly to benefit from your knowledge and experience faster and be prepared to pay for it. You need to decide how you facilitate those different groups. Do you provide additional coaching (either 1:1 or in group format)? Do you have a recurring online or offline membership? Do you have digital resources and training that allow you to dive deeper into your methodologies while maintaining leverage and time freedom?

The goal becomes establishing and growing a relationship with your readers that has the ability to develop over time while you move your customer incrementally closer to whatever outcome they are seeking. It's no longer transactionally about how many books you have sold, where you don't even know who those people are. Instead, you are identifying those people and nurturing them by saying, *"You are my customer now. I want to serve you at the highest level I can. What else can I do to help you?"*

Books are no longer just an entity in themselves. In the new digital world we find ourselves living in, books are the first step into the ecosystem of potential products and services only limited by your imagination. Once you begin thinking about it in this way, your book has the ability to transform into a 7-figure business overnight.

CHAPTER 3

UNLOCKING THE FORMULA

When my client, Jordan Platten, first came to me, he had already built a successful social media marketing agency and had created an online learning program around showing others how to do the same. Although he was already doing very well, Jordan had huge aspirations and was hungry for growth, not just in the financial sense but also for growing his credibility and authority within the marketplace.

I could tell immediately that he was not in this to make a quick buck. He wanted to make an impact and actually help people. And if you're looking for a formula for success, don't underestimate that as a rock-solid starting point.

We agreed that he should release a book based on his knowledge and what he'd been able to achieve by building this business model. This would elevate his status within the marketplace and could be used as a tool to identify the ideal customers for his premium online course and upcoming live events.

Jordan was confident that if he had a consistent and reliable way to get his book into the hands of his dream customers, they'd immediately see the opportunity in what he was offering and want to work with him more closely. But with just two products (the book and the course), he was unsure how this could be structured into a high-converting book funnel.

I explained to Jordan that the ultimate success of any book funnel comes down to 3 distinct phases: **Acquire**, **Liquidate** and **Ascend**.

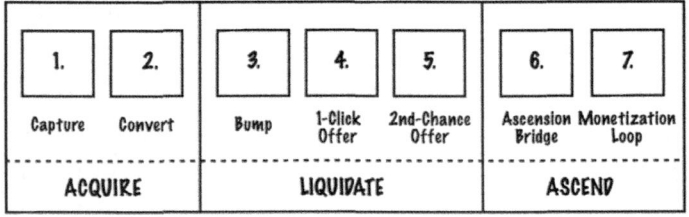

Phase 1 is the Acquire phase. It allows you to control the amount of visitors being exposed to your book while capturing and segmenting the data of both your book buyers as well as those who did not yet convert to purchase.

This was great for Jordan, as he'd know exactly who was purchasing his book and be able to speak to them directly through his various marketing channels. He could also follow up with those who didn't complete their purchase, through automated emails, to discover what objections his potential readers had and pivot his messaging to address and overcome them.

Phase 2 is the Liquidate phase. This is where you immediately offer your book buyers the opportunity to upgrade their purchase to include additional items just like Amazon does, except now you can offer your own products and services instead of someone else's.

Jordan understood the premise of providing additional upgrades at the point of sale to increase the average value of each new customer, but he was a little stuck on what to offer. He had his main learning program that he ultimately wanted his readers to ascend into, but it was a big jump from just purchasing a book.

Just like you wouldn't get down on one knee and propose marriage on a first date, at this stage you're not looking to go all in and immediately offer your new reader your most expensive product or service.

You want them to get to know you, trust in your ideas and methodologies, and establish a desire to want to do future business with you by solving their immediate problems.

I learned this process from my friend and mentor, Dean Holland. Dean explained that although everyone talks about products providing solutions to a problem, what they often don't see is how purchasing any product actually opens up a new set of problems for that customer.

Think about your backyard. It's in a bit of a mess and there's nowhere for your kids to play, so you think, "Let's lay down some turf to create a lawn here." You have a vision of being outside with your family on a hot summer day with the grill on having a BBQ and the kids rolling around on the beautiful lawn without care in the world.

Problem solved right? But what happens next when the grass starts to grow? You can bet that your next purchase is almost certainly going to be a lawnmower. You previously had no need or desire for one, but all of a sudden it becomes an essential purchase because you now have grass in your yard, and it's growing daily.

And what about maintaining that mower? After the first cut, you find yourself needing to clean it out, and you need the proper tools. Each purchase, although solving the problem it was intended to, naturally opens up a new problem that needs to be solved to be able to reach your Oz (that vision of the perfect family day in the yard cooking up burgers).

This is just human purchase behavior. The secret to knowing what to offer your customers next is to **solve the new problem that was created by whatever was purchased on the previous step.** I urge you to take a second and reread that sentence, as it's one of the most powerful lessons in online marketing.

This concept is known as offer sequencing. You can do this for yourself by creating one or more "micro products" that easily complement your book but are specifically engineered to cultivate your readers into dream customers by providing them with the logical next step that solves their new problem and creates a sense of urgency that naturally primes them for your core product offerings.

So how did we apply this concept to Jordan's book funnel? In his book, The 15 Minute Agency, Jordan shows total beginners how they can achieve financial and time freedom by helping business owners run advertising campaigns on their social media. That can be established as the "WHAT." So naturally, any subsequent product offerings would be based around showing "HOW" to implement on the "WHAT."

Jordan knew from his own personal experience that the biggest problem his reader would face after reading the book would be signing his or her first client. He remembered how intimidating it was the first time around and how unprepared he was, but he knew that once he gained the confidence to sign up his first client, the second, third and fourth became much easier. He also knew that if his readers had some income coming in from what he was teaching, they would be far more likely to purchase his full program. They just needed that first client to get the ball rolling.

So Jordan created his first liquidator microproduct: a bundle of the exact template scripts and contracts he uses to sign up clients for his own social media marketing agency. This was a simple collection of PDF files that could be automatically delivered to the customer via email immediately after purchase without any additional work on Jordan's part. It was simple for him to create. In fact, he already had all of the pieces in place in his own business, but more important was the value this provided to the reader.

The reader purchases the book to hear about Jordan's new opportunity with social media marketing. That creates a desire within them to achieve financial and time freedom just like Jordan has. By purchasing the book, they are literally buying into the concept, and now their mind naturally switches to, *"How can I do this for myself?"* That automatically establishes the new problem in their mind as, *"If I could just get started by signing up one client."* Jordan's bundle is equipping them with the tools to solve that next logical problem and get them closer to their Oz of overarching financial freedom through the business model.

But it doesn't stop there. By providing the tools and confidence to sign client number one, Jordan solves that big first problem for his reader so in their mind that itch has been scratched. Again from personal experience, he knows that having clients is only profitable if they stay with you month on month, and for them to do that, you need to get them excellent results. So naturally, his next offer would be a product training on how to get results for your clients FAST (the next logical step and the next big problem).

Having this logical story of progression throughout the steps in his funnel meant that these additional offers became a no-brainer to a percentage of his readers. Not everyone will take action and upgrade. But those who do take action will increase the average transaction value or average cart value, meaning every customer on average becomes worth more to Jordan and his business, allowing him to scale faster and more predictability with, in effect, an unlimited advertising budget (more on that in the next chapter).

This process of offer sequencing has multiple benefits. Not only does it solidify your credibility and authority as the expert by showing that you understand the journey that your reader is on but it also importantly installs buying beliefs into your audience by asking them to make a series of micro commitments.

If you're not familiar with the term "micro commitments," it is a very powerful persuasion technique based on Robert Cialdini's commitment and consistency principle, which suggests people have a hard-wired desire to be consistent even after the original incentive or motivation is no longer present. Essentially, instead of outright asking your prospect to make one big decision, you break it up into smaller decisions to increase the likelihood you'll get your main objective accomplished.

By purchasing your "micro-products," your reader is more likely to want to work with you or your business in the future.

Don't worry if you feel you don't have anything suitable to offer here yet. We'll discuss each of the 3 liquidator stages in detail with additional examples later in this book.

The important takeaway here is that successful book funnels making five and six figures per month are not a random sequence of steps, nor a series of random products offered after the book. There's a very specific formula of progression, not just between the steps but across the entire funnel sequence.

The biggest mistake I see with book funnels that are struggling to convert is they don't get this one key concept of offer sequencing. If you already have a book funnel that is not converting, it's likely this is the missing piece of the puzzle that literally ties it all together.

When you can align the story of progression with the success path of your ideal reader, then each individual offer becomes the perfect next step for your customer, and your conversion rates will soar.

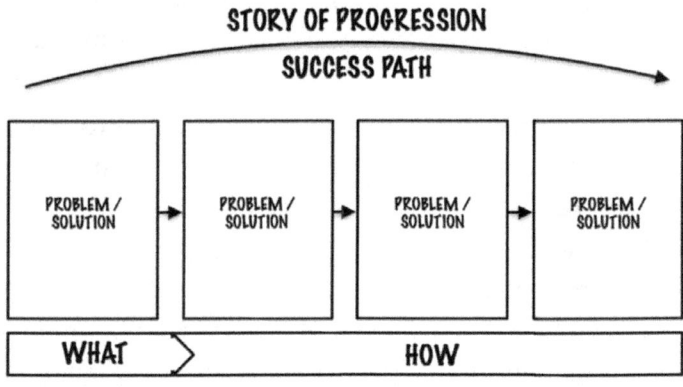

Phase 3 is the Ascend phase. You want to expose your book buyers to your primary desired action, i.e., complete an application, request a sales call, join a membership, etc., and continue to build that relationship with them to set them on their success path towards Oz.

Jordan knew that at least initially, he wanted to ascend his readers up to join his online learning program as he knew that's where they could get the best results in the shortest time frame possible. But also, by staying in contact with those customers through email and other marketing channels, he could invite them to his upcoming live events when the time came.

Not only that but he could also look for partners in his industry that may have other additional products or services that could serve his readers and strike deals with them to earn a commission on his referral. This is known as joint ventures and affiliate marketing.

We'll break down exactly what goes into each phase and how to implement them for yourself in part 2 of this book, Book Funnel Building Blocks.

Failure to either understand or implement just 1 of the 3 phases can result in an ineffective campaign. That's the bad news. The good news is that if you are not seeing success, compartmentalizing the formula into these 3 distinct phases makes it very simple to identify which aspect is not performing well and quickly fix it. This simplicity drives action, and action drives results.

CHAPTER 4

THE MOST IMPORTANT METRIC

While the world of sales funnels and digital marketing often requires you to navigate through confusing terminology, industry jargon and complicated metrics, the great news is a successful book funnel relies only on a single equation containing three simple metrics:

1. Cost Per Acquisition (CPA)

This is the amount of paid advertising it takes to acquire a new book buyer. For example, if you spend $100 on advertising and you sell 5 books, your Cost Per Acquisition is $20.

Total advertising spend ($100) ÷ total number of books sold (5) = $20 CPA.

2. Fulfillment Cost Per Order (FCPO)

This is the amount it costs you to print and ship your book to your customer's front door.

You may use an external fulfillment center that both prints and ships your book (examples of these services are provided later in this book), or you may already have your books printed and decide to only outsource the order fulfillment.

You might even wish to fulfill your book orders yourself, however, I don't recommend this approach unless you already have the infrastructure in place, as it pays to have this aspect as automated as possible.

Your FCPO will depend on your supplier, the size and weight of your book, the packaging and shipping methods you select plus economies of scale. The bottom line here is the more books you print and ship, the lower your costs will be.

Take for example: it costs you $5 to print your book and $5 for shipping and handling, your FCPO would be $10.

3. Average Cart Value (ACV)

This is the total amount, on average, that a new customer spends when they purchase your book.

If a new customer purchased your book on your website for $15, then your Average Cart Value would always be $15.

However, when a new customer purchases your book from your book funnel, they are offered a sequence of complementary offers to enhance their experience and advance their learning. These inlude:

- Order Bump
- One-Click Offer (often multiple)
- Second-Chance Offer

We'll discuss each of these offer types in detail within the upcoming chapters and how, on average, a certain percentage of customers will purchase each of these additional offers provided they meet specific criteria. This means that when selling your book using a book funnel, you have the potential for a much higher average cart value than if you sold the same book on a traditional website.

For example: If, on average, for every 100 books you sell to new customers, 30 of those new customers check the box to add a $37 order bump offer to their order during checkout, the result would be as follows:

- Total additional revenue generated: $37 x 30 = $1,110.
- $1,110 ÷ 100 customers = $11.10 additional revenue per customer.
- Original Average Cart Value: $15
- New Average Cart Value: $15 + $11.10 = $26.50

That's just with one Order Bump! Imagine what happens when you give your customers the opportunity to purchase multiple higher-priced products from you immediately after they purchase your book.

Now show those same 100 customers a One-Click Offer as an "upsell" immediately after purchase, and on average, 15% choose to upgrade for $97.

- Total additional revenue generated: $97 x 15 = $1,455
- $1,455 ÷ 100 customers = $14.55 additional revenue per customer.
- Original Average Cart Value: $15
- New Average Cart Value: $15 + $11.10 + $14.55 = $40.65

You just increased the revenue generated from your book by 170%.

It's not uncommon that by combining multiple additional offers into your funnel flow, you can increase your Average Cart Value as high as $45 to $50 on the front end.

That means, on average, you can now potentially make $45 back for every book put out into the marketplace, minus your costs. And if you've been paying attention, you'll notice that means you can now actually get paid to generate brand new, highly qualified customers from paid advertising.

CHAPTER 5

ACTIVATING YOUR UNLIMITED ADVERTISING BUDGET

Now that we know which three metrics are most important to book funnel success, let's look at how they fit together into *The Book Funnel Formula* (BFF) Equation.

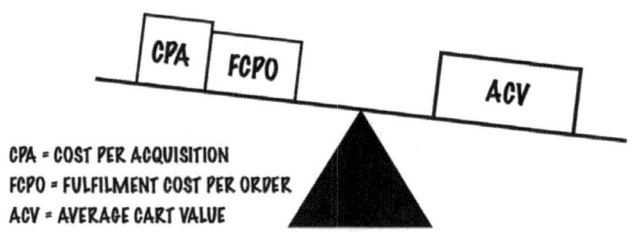

Cost Per Acquisition + Fulfillment Cost Per Order ≤ Average Cart Value

Advertising spend to sell 1 book + cost to fulfill that order needs to be less than or equal to the average total amount the customer spends during the initial transaction. The goal here is to break even on the front end. However, if done correctly, you can make a nice profit from every new customer you bring into your business.

When I refer to the "front end," I'm talking about the initial sequence of steps a new customer goes through during their initial book purchase. This consists of the primary book purchase plus the opportunity for your customer to upgrade to your liquidator micro-products which we'll discuss further in the Liquidation section of this book.

Once you get this right, it becomes a self-perpetuating cycle and one that easily scales quickly and beautifully. The money simply moves in a circle and creates the effect of an unlimited advertising budget since it's constantly replenishing itself. **This is the holy grail of online advertising.**

Every time you spend $1 on advertising, you're getting at least $1 back while acquiring a buying customer to whom you can sell more stuff, including your higher-ticket services.

Once you achieve this self-perpetuating cycle, you'll want to invest as many dollars as you can because you'll be acquiring new highly qualified buyers into your business at zero cost. Using this

method, you have the potential to get your book into the hands of more readers than you may ever have thought possible.

Luckily, the BFF equation simplifies the entire marketing process because you only have 3 metrics to monitor and improve at any given time.

If your book funnel is not breaking even on the front end or you want it to become more profitable, you know you need to either increase your ACV or reduce your CPA or FCPO.

That's it! Now that you understand the numbers and what it takes to be successful, let's look at how to create your very own Book Funnel using The *Book Funnel Formula*.

In the following section, I'm going to show you behind the scenes of the 3 core phases of *The Book Funnel Formula* and break down the key components of each so you have a full understanding of how they work together.

PART 2

BOOK FUNNEL
BUILDING BLOCKS

"Gary is the industry expert when it comes to creating a book funnel that works. Having a booking funnel is kind of like getting clients for free. Who wouldn't want that? His help, expertise and understanding of how all the components fit together is priceless. If you want to leverage your information in the best way, get Gary to help you. I paid Gary for his top-end consultation fee and he was worth every penny. If you see this review on his book or on his site, buy whatever he is selling. It will be a great investment for you. Thanks Gary, I appreciate all you do for us."

Ed J. C. Smith—Author, Psychologist, Serial Entrepreneur and Founder of Champion Academy

CHAPTER 6

THE 3 CORE PHASES

As I have said before, it is my sincerest belief that you, as the author, should be in control of the book sales process, and you should be able to communicate directly with your reader to offer them more value through an ecosystem of highly profitable, targeted products and services, without the traditional restrictions of mainstream publishers, online marketplaces and retailers.

Now that you have discovered the 3 phases of *The Book Funnel Formula* (Acquire, Liquidate, Ascend) and understand the overarching story of progression that ties these together in parallel with the success path of your reader, it's time to dive deeper and uncover the exact elements you need to create your own high-converting book funnel.

As you've already seen in the diagram, I've broken these elements down into 7 unique building blocks to make the process simple and superfast for you to implement.

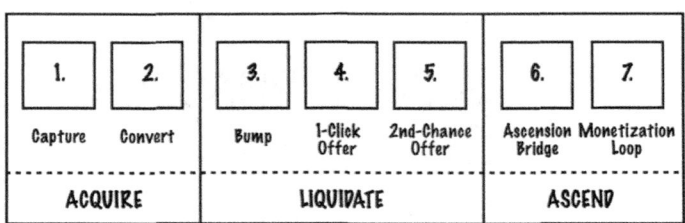

While I would love the opportunity to work with you on all this (assuming we are a good fit), you can take these building blocks and use them for yourself. Just remember, the fastest way to success is to have an experienced expert (e.g., a coach, consultant, advisor) to guide, prompt, question, challenge and encourage you. More details on how we can work together can be found in part 3, starting on page 111.

CHAPTER 7

PHASE 1: ACQUIRE

Phase 1 is designed to identify high-quality leads that are predisposed to your credibility in the marketplace as an established author and convert them into customers.

The goal here is to effectively communicate the idea of why someone should want to read your book and give them a reason to take action now. Typically this will take the form of a longer form page that contains images, text, a video, and often an order form.

Once created, you can use this page as a hub for all of your book-marketing efforts, linking back to it from all kinds of sources like blog posts, online videos, paid advertising, your website's homepage, podcast & media interviews, etc.

I refer to this initial step as the **Acquire** phase, as it has two objectives:

1. **Capture** visitor information as a lead (identify interest)
2. **Convert** those leads into book buyers

IDENTIFY INTEREST

As you can see from the image, the first page in your book funnel (known as a "landing page" or "sales page") is constructed in a very specific format to increase the number of visitors that take action before choosing to leave the page.

Unlike a traditional page on a website, landing pages deliberately have no navigation bar and no links to additional pages. This is to completely focus the visitor's attention on the offer in front of them and reduce the opportunities for distraction, subsequently resulting in a higher conversion rate.

Typically the top portion of the page (known as "above the fold") consists of a headline section that describes the primary benefit or outcome that a reader would obtain from consuming the book. Underneath the headline, to the left of the page, there is a sales video that further emphasizes the main benefits of the book while positioning the author as an expert in their industry.

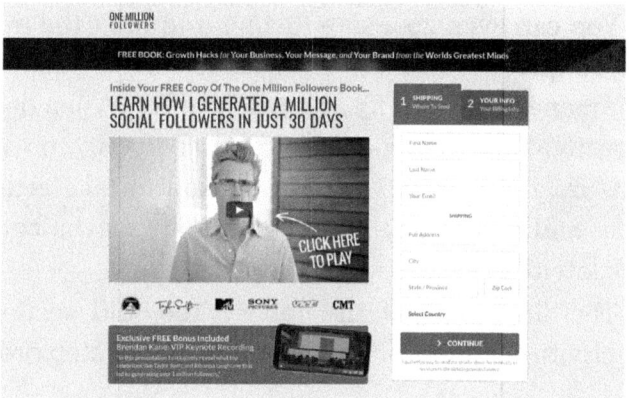

It's important to realize that on this page you not only communicate the idea of why the visitor should want to read your book but you also need to give them a reason to take action now. If your book is available on Amazon, for instance, how do you prevent them from opening up a new tab and purchasing the book there (instantly losing your control over the sales process)?

The solution comes with differentiating the offer to make it unique. You can do this by including a digital bonus or bonuses that aren't available anywhere else. In the image above, you can see that my client, Brendan Kane, offers his book buyers an exclusive recording of a keynote presentation. This bonus is not available anywhere else, and therefore, differentiates the value proposition, giving the visitor a reason to purchase specifically through the funnel to receive the bonus content.

even go a step further and limit the time quantity of these bonuses to further increase the urgency and scarcity around the offer. When done correctly, this can massively increase your conversions by giving your visitors a reason to take action today and not just think about it and "maybe come back later."

The final part of the "above the fold section" directly to the right of the video is the two-step order form.

This is a tried-and-tested format used by many well-known online marketers because it is responsive to how a visitor will interact with the page.

The psychology behind this page design format is simple. When a visitor lands on the page, the headline will intrigue or excite them enough to click to play the video. Then while watching the video, they can simultaneously begin filling out their information on the first step of the two-step order form which asks, *"Where should we send your book?"*

When I first saw these two-step order forms, I would have presumed that the conversions would be terrible as they are asking for 8+ fields of information, yet because of the psychology of how it's laid out, it's not unrealistic to have 30% to 40% of all visitors that view the page submit their information on that first step.

Check out the stats from this step...

	Page Views		Opt-Ins	
	All	Uniques	All	Rate
🛒 Order Form	39,773	31,511	11,549	36.65%

Being able to so easily obtain this level of visitor-to-lead conversion rate is fantastic because it's equal to what we'd expect to see on a traditional online squeeze page where something of value is offered in return for an email address.

The difference though is the first step collects not only an email address (which could, of course, be faked) but also captures a full breakdown of customer information, including full name, email address, phone number and full shipping address. It's also unlikely that someone would input fake information here because then they could not physically receive their book, and we'd have no way of contacting them about their order, so we are getting a similar conversion rate on a higher quality of lead.

Below the "continue" button which takes the visitor to the second step of the order form where they can enter their card details, is a disclaimer that shows by clicking this button the visitor consents to receive your future marketing materials. Therefore, when a visitor clicks the button, their information is automatically captured and sent to your CRM or marketing automation software. Then if those people don't purchase the book immediately, you now have the ability to follow up with them directly via email, phone or even direct mail.

This allows you to quickly begin developing a highly qualified database of leads that have already shown interest in your book. You can then use your CRM or autoresponder software to automatically follow up with those people to encourage them to complete their pending book purchase, known as an "abandon cart" sequence, or add them to your weekly newsletter sequence to build rapport before presenting them with additional offers for your products or services that may be a better fit for them.

Once you have captured the visitor data on step one of the two-step order form, the next aim is to **convert** that interest into a book purchase.

CONVERTING THE SALE

As we said earlier, the measure of an ideal customer is that they are both willing and able to pay for your assistance. It's now time to get those dream customers to raise their hand and identify themselves in the form of pulling out their credit card to purchase your book.

Naturally, we want as many visitors as possible to purchase the book on this page, as the more people that purchase, the higher the conversion rate and the lower the cost of acquisition from paid advertising.

With that in mind, you have two options for how you offer the book to your customer:

1. Physical copy
2. Digital copy

Personally I love offering the physical copy to customers, as a physical book tends to have a greater perceived value than a digital book or "eBook." There's also something magical about the future relationship with a customer who actually has a physical copy of your book at their home or in their office, especially if you go on to have a call with them to discuss your additional products and services.

When you take up shelf space alongside their favorite, well-established authors, it instantly boosts your credibility and your perceived authority. And if you have implemented the three phases of *The Book Funnel Formula* correctly, by the time their book is delivered, you will already have built an intimate relationship with them to the point that they feel that they know, and more importantly, trust you.

While getting your customers to complete their purchase within your sales funnel allows you to capture the full customer details and create a list of highly qualified proven buyers that you can begin to expose to higher-ticket products and services using online methods like email marketing and retargeting (more on that later in this book), shipping a physical copy to your customer directly circumvents the noisy, instant gratification world of the internet and takes the relationship offline where you can benefit from more of the customer's focused attention.

This is a great place to include additional marketing materials, either within or in addition to your book, encouraging your customer to take action on working with you more closely after reading, as they will be consuming these materials without the usual online distractions.

Free + Shipping

In order to get your book into the hands of as many of your ideal customers as possible, you may want to make a Free + Shipping offer. This is where you are advertising the book for free, either for a short or prolonged period, and all the visitor needs to do is pay the shipping and handling charge to receive it. This is powerful because you have the ability to use the most powerful word in marketing: "Free."

Now bear with me a second here. I know after all the effort you went through to create your book, the idea of giving it away for free may seem daunting or that it somehow devalues its credibility, but this couldn't be further from the truth. I am about to show you how offering your book for free can actually make you more profitable and allow you to scale much faster. Let me explain...

When interacting with people on social media or running online advertising, the idea is to make the purchase of your book as attractive and enticing as possible. A Free + Shipping offer lowers the barrier to entry for someone to get your book, but you are still asking them to make a micro-commitment by pulling out their credit card to pay the shipping charge on step two of the two-step order form. This is important because by initiating that purchase, they are much more likely to continue to buy from you.

As you can see from the image on the next page the customer enters their details for the free book while the shipping & handling charge is added to their order automatically before they checkout.

GARY WHITE

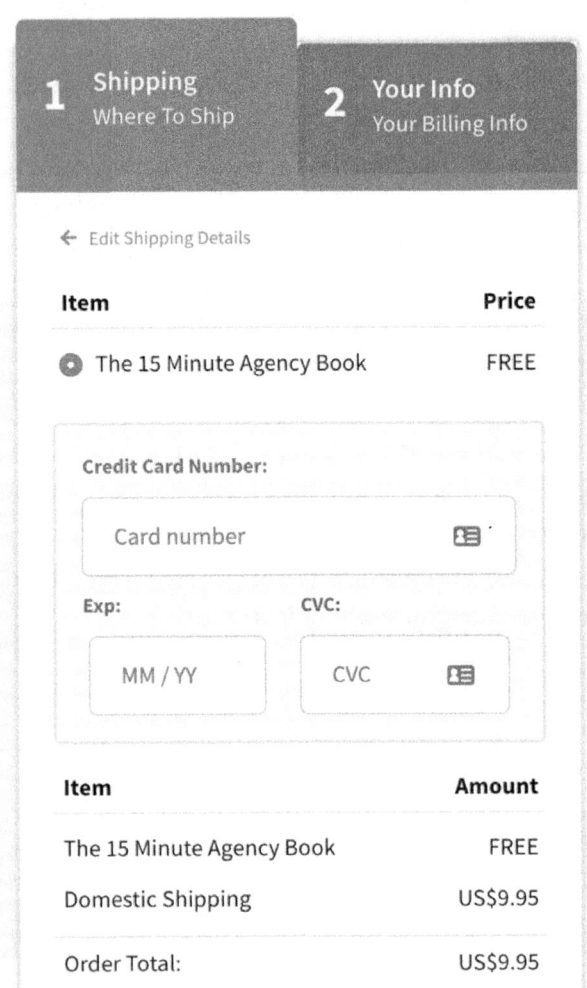

The main reason many of the world's top online marketers use the Free + Shipping model over just charging for a physical copy of the book is because they know that this is a proven method to increase the conversion rate on the Acquire phase.

They understand that by increasing the conversion rate on the book, not only does this increase the amount of books that go into the hands of their ideal customers from the same amount of visitors coming to their landing page but it also directly impacts how much money they will make throughout the entirety of the funnel.

The diagram below shows how a typical book funnel might likely perform when selling the book on the front end for $9.95. With no mention of the word "FREE," the first step in the funnel converts at 5%, so for every 1,000 visitors that see the page, 50 of them go on to purchase the book. That means that 50 people continue through the funnel to see the additional offers in the Liquidate phase.

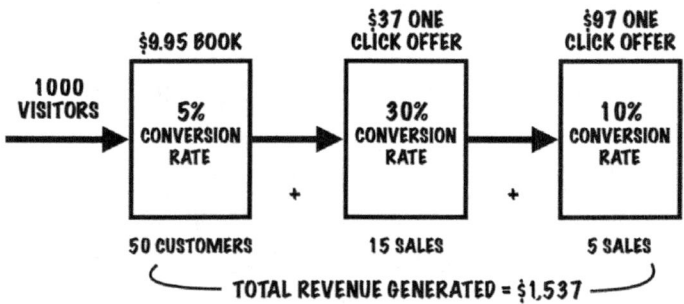

If 50 people see the subsequent One-Click Offer for $37 (which we will discuss in detail later in this section) and it converts at 30%, then that will result in 15 sales and $555.00 in additional revenue.

If the same 50 people continue to a second One-Click Offer, this time priced at $97 and that converts at 10%, then that will generate 5 sales and an additional $485.00 in revenue.

This totals $1,537 in revenue from 1,000 visitors.

Now let's take a look at how the same funnel would perform if we changed nothing but the conversion rate on the front end by introducing a Free + Shipping model.

By using the power of the word "Free" in our marketing, the first step in the funnel now converts at 10% (typically our target conversion rate on a free + shipping book).

	Page Views		Opt-Ins		Sales		
	All	Uniques	All	Rate	Count	Rate	Value
🛒 Order Form	2,695	2,239	826	36.89%	210	9.38%	$2,771.50

So for every 1,000 visitors that see the page, 100 of them go on to purchase the book. That means that now 100 people continue through the funnel to see the additional offers in the Liquidate phase.

Now without changing anything else in the funnel, all the other conversion rates and price points stay exactly the same. Let's take a look at what happens.

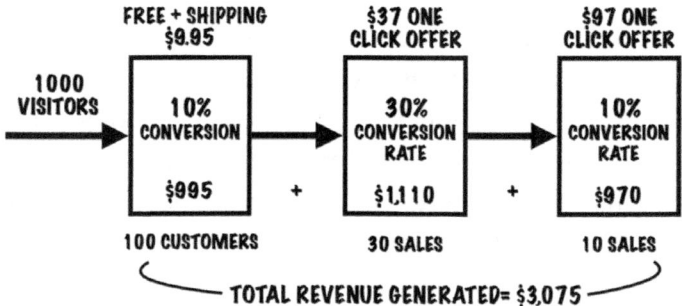

If 100 people now see the subsequent One-Click Offer for $37 and it still converts at the same 30%, then that will result in 30 sales and a huge $1,110.00 in additional revenue.

If the same 100 people now continue to a second One-Click Offer, priced exactly the same at $97 and that still converts at 10%, then that will generate 10 sales and an additional $970.00 in revenue.

That means the total revenue from the same 1,000 visitors is now $3,075. You just doubled revenue across the entire funnel just by increasing that one variable. That is the power of a Free + Shipping offer.

Of course, the downside of offering a physical book is that you have hard fulfillment costs to print and ship that book out to your customer. Costs here can be minimized by printing copies in bulk and limiting the weight of your book by only sending paperback copies, but it's important that you are able to cover your costs on the front end.

I recommend you do not handle the fulfillment of your books yourself, as it can act as a distraction and time suck when you should be concentrating your efforts solely on the marketing of your book.

This is extremely easy to outsource these days and should not feel daunting. There are numerous done-for-you fulfilment companies who will take delivery of your printed books and store them, then ship them out on your behalf for every order that comes in through your funnel. All completely automated without you lifting a finger.

Some of my preferred fulfilment vendors are:

- eCommerceFulfilment.com
- MailEverything.com
- Acutrack.com

While the first two examples will store and ship your books for you if you already have them printed elsewhere, Acutrack will handle the entire process for you by actually printing and shipping your books, thus providing an all-in-one solution.

You can reach out to Acutrack at:

Acutrack.com/get-a-quote citing 'Book Funnel Formula' to save an additional $199 off your fulfilment quote.

If you feel that you want to utilize the benefits of a book funnel but do not want to worry about the fulfilment aspect of shipping books, then the alternative is to use your book funnel to sell digital copies in the form of an eBook.

While this method limits some of the potential benefits talked about above, the immediate and obvious benefit is you are removing your FCPO (Fulfillment Cost Per Order) from the BFF Equation, so it's somewhat easier to "balance the scale," meaning your ACV (Average Cart Value) does not need to be as high to break even or become profitable.

This can be a highly effective method for beginners to implement, as the barrier to entry is lower, and there is one less variable to measure.

"We spent hundreds of hours on our book and all of its added value pieces, and it was amazing bringing it to life with Gary's help. Not only were we excited about learning and growing with this process, but every single sale brought us invaluable data. Gary did a fantastic job of walking us through what worked and what didn't, and we gained a deeper understanding of who our audience was and why they bought our book. Our book was our passion, and we are so grateful for the work and attention Gary put in to help us share it with the world."

**Jason Forrest—Speaker, Award-Winning Author
and CEO of Forrest Performance Group
[Inc. 5000 Fastest-Growing Private Company]**

CHAPTER 8

PHASE 2: LIQUIDATE

Now that you have identified those visitors that have shown interest in your book and looked at how to convert the highest percentage of them into book sales, let's move on to look at how to increase your Average Cart Value (the dollar amount, on average, that each book sale is worth) by making additional offers that:

1. Provide greater convenience and value to the reader.
2. Allow you to immediately liquidate your marketing costs.
3. Prime your reader to want to do future business with you.

This is where being in control of your own sales process really starts to get exciting because instead of

Amazon offering additional products to your customers without providing you with any additional income, you now get to offer YOUR OWN additional products and services to your customers, and you get to keep all the profits.

I believe by putting the author in control of the sales process, this model is the future of selling books online. And by implementing this yourself now, you have the opportunity to be ahead of the curve.

So how do you offer additional upgrades to your customer at the point of purchase without seeming pushy or sounding like a sleazy salesperson? How do you know exactly what to offer your customers that will truly enhance their experience and increase the likelihood of them doing future business with you?

In this section, we'll look in detail at the 3 steps of liquidation offers and how they ultimately fit into the big picture of *The Book Funnel Formula*.

THE CLOSEST THING TO FREE MONEY

What if you could literally double the revenue generated from your book offer simply by adding an additional 2–3 sentences to your order form?

Would you do it? I'm guessing, unless you hate money, the answer is yes!

While it sounds almost too good to be true, this is in fact perfectly possible using what's called an Order Form Bump, otherwise known as an "Order Bump."

This is an additional opportunity presented to customers right at the point of purchase that can be accepted or declined using a simple checkbox. This checkbox is displayed on step two of the Two-Step Order Form underneath the credit card details.

> ☐ **Yes Brian, Upgrade My Order!**
>
> **Coaching Conversation Secrets:** Want an 80% Discount on One of Our Best Selling Products?
>
> This Special Report will give you **"11 Insider Secrets Guaranteed to Transform Your Team's Performance"**... helping you to **DOUBLE your results** and **HALF the time.**
>
> **PLUS** You will also get instant access to the **audio book of The Weekly Coaching Conversation** so you can start listening right away.
>
> Check YES above to add this special offer to your order now for just ~~$197~~ $37. (This offer is not available at any other time or place.)
>
> **63% Of Our Most Successful Members Choose This Upgrade...**

The position of this offer is very strategic, as the customer has not yet fully committed to the purchase but has made enough micro-commitments (entering shipping info on step one and entering credit card information on step two to have a vested interest in completing the sale.

The Order Bump upgrade is only available with the purchase of the book, and therefore, if the customer wanted another chance to upgrade, they would need to repurchase the book again. This psychology means if the offer is strong enough and fits the criteria listed later in the section, there is a high likelihood that the customer will take the opportunity to upgrade right there and then.

This is often seen as a "no-brainer offer" where the perceived value is high but the price point is low, and the benefit to the customer either delivers greater convenience or the ability to obtain faster results.

The most compelling and highest-converting order bumps are for products that do not require much in the way of explanation (as space for text is limited). A powerful way to harness this is to change the medium of the information without changing the concept the customer has already embraced and bought into.

A simple method to achieve this is to offer either the digital or audio versions of the book for an additional upgrade fee. This is super simple to implement, as it allows you to give greater value to your customer without requiring any additional effort on your part.

If you are selling a physical book as your main offer, you can frame the digital access as an opportunity to get started right now without needing to wait for the book to ship to begin consuming the content. This is the ultimate convenience for the customer and also gives them access to the content sooner, therefore, accelerating their results.

In our testing, we find that although the digital access opportunity converts very well, we were somewhat capped by the amount we could charge per unit, as customers already had a preconceived notion of how much an eBook or audiobook should cost, should they purchase it on Audible or a similar platform.

In order to maximize the average cart value on every transaction, we wanted to be able to raise the price point, and therefore, had to differentiate the offer so it was no longer directly comparable to the offer on other platforms. Through the process of testing, we found that by bundling your eBook or audiobook with additional digital content in the form of videos or PDFs, we were able to increase the price point of the offer from $19 to $47 without reducing the conversion rate, meaning that we make more money on average for every book sold.

I recommend NOT bundling any additional physical items that require shipping into your Order Bump offer so that you can maximize the profit generated from each sale.

The great thing about these offers is you only need to create them once, and they will pay you again and again, time after time without any additional work on your behalf while delivering greater convenience to your customers and the ability for them to obtain faster results.

What could you offer as an Order Bump with the sale of your book? Do you already have a digital or audio version? How could you differentiate the offer to maximize revenue and conversions?

For more information on creating a high-converting order bump, go to:

TheBookFunnelFormula.com/launch

SOLVING THE NEXT PROBLEM

After someone purchases your book, they are automatically redirected to the next page.

A typical author selling their book on a traditional website would take their new customer directly to a thank you page to confirm the purchase. While this has been the status quo for many years, this method leaves a huge amount of opportunity on the table, both for you and your customer.

Instead, a savvy author who understands *The Book Funnel Formula* knows that when someone is making any purchase, they are psychologically in "buying mode" and more likely to purchase additional items right there and then, than at any other time.

With that in mind, rather than to close the "purchase loop" in the customer's mind, you want to give book buyers the opportunity to upgrade their order right at the moment that you and your book are at the forefront of their mind. We do this using a method called the One-Click Offer.

A One-Click Offer is an exclusive page that is shown only to buyers of your book immediately after they purchase with a one-time opportunity to upgrade their existing order.

This concept is particularly powerful because at this stage in the process, the customer has already entered their billing information on the previous step, so you can allow them to upgrade their order, normally including a large discount by clicking a single button rather than requiring them to fill out all of their information again. This reduces the friction within the sales process and increases the convenience for the customer, therefore, raising the conversion rate, meaning more book buyers go on to upgrade to your One-Click Offer, and you increase your revenue per book sold.

In the image below, you can see that nearly 20% of book buyers went on to upgrade their order for an additional $67, generating an additional $19,497 in revenue.

	Page Views		Opt-Ins			Sales	
	All	Uniques	All	Rate	Count	Rate	Value
🛒 Order Form	27,120	18,912	10,715	56.66%	1,870	9.89%	$27,449....
↑ OTO 1	1,874	1,541	363	23.56%	291	18.88%	$19,497....

How much money are you potentially leaving on the table without a One-Click Offer in place?

Once you see the power of this concept and the additional revenue it can generate, it seems madness that any author would not be using this method.

Inevitably, one of the first questions I always get asked when breaking down this process is, *"So how much should I charge for my one-click offer?"*

While there are some price points that I have seen greater success with than others, like the $67 above, really this is asking the wrong question. The secret to a high-converting One-Click Offer which successfully and sustainably increases your overall average cart value is not based on how much you charge but on the problem that you solve.

When someone purchases your book, it's because they have an itch. As soon as they order the book (even before they receive it, if it's a physical copy), in their mind they have scratched that itch. There is never any reason for them to ever buy information related to that thing again (especially in the next 30 seconds) because they believe that your book will scratch that itch.

Just like in Jordan Platten's example earlier in this book, you do not want to go on offering more of the same thing that scratches the same itch. Instead, you want to solve the new problem that was created by whatever was purchased on the previous step.

Once you can implement this effectively, you will be able to charge more for your One-Click Offer while retaining a steady conversion rate.

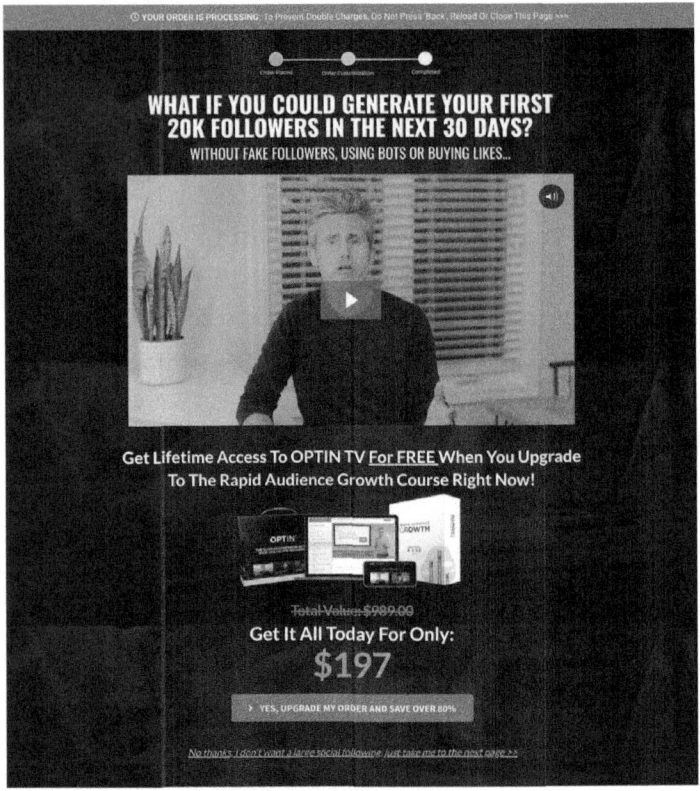

As you can see from the image above, the first step on any One-Click Offer page is to keep the "buying loop" open. While customers in some markets are often preconditioned to the concept of sales funnels, your audience may not be. This means you need to make it completely clear that the purchase session is still open and ongoing.

With that in mind, it's important not to begin with a headline that says "Thank You For Your Order" because your customer may mistakenly presume they have completed their purchase and can now exit the page.

If the customer feels it's now okay to get distracted, they may immediately head to their inbox to look for their receipt, leaving the page to potentially never return. This can result in a needless drop in conversions.

The job of the headline is to get the customer to watch the video and consume the rest of the information on the page. This is a "make or break" feature of the page, as it's directly responsible for someone either sticking around to hear your sales message or deciding they are not interested in what else you have to say.

You can even set up your software to show different headlines to different buyers, allowing you to test what works best and which combination results in the most sales.

Below the video is a clear option for the customer to either accept or decline their upgrade opportunity with a single click. It's important that this is a binary yes/no decision because if there are too many options or too much to think about, it leads to indecision and can kill conversions.

Although we discovered this through rigorous testing, there is a scientific name for this effect, known as "overchoice." The term was first introduced by Alvin Toffler in his 1970 book, Future Shock, where he found that people have a difficult time making a decision when faced with many options. You've likely experienced this phenomenon yourself.

How many times have you found yourself scrolling through Netflix trying to find something to watch? I find myself doing this, and 15 minutes later I often end up just closing the app feeling frustrated. Yet back in the "old days," I would happily put a tv channel on and stick with it because what was shown was decided for me.

This same psychology works in your sales process. Having too many equally good options is mentally draining because each option must be weighed against alternatives to select the best one. If your customer has to think too hard about which option to choose, they will generally leave the decision "for later" and abandon the process.

Of course, not everyone will accept your opportunity to upgrade, and that's ok. By providing a clear method for your customers to decline your offer, you can easily take them to the next page in your process, whether that be a confirmation page or an additional One-Click Offer.

Once you see the power of the One-Click Offer, you may want to begin offering your book buyers multiple options to upgrade. While this is good practice, I normally limit my One-Click Offers to 2, to avoid making the customer's journey too long, uncomfortable or overly salesy.

If you decide to implement more than 1 One-Click Offer, it's important to make the page designs visually different from each other so that your customers can very easily tell that they have been taken to a new page with a brand new one-time offer.

Do you already have a digital product that fits the criteria for a One-Click Offer? Could you modify or splinter part of your existing offers? Or what could you easily create that serves your audience while priming them for your core offer?

For more information on creating high-converting One-Click Offers, go to:

TheBookFunnelFormula.com/launch

SQUEEZING THE ORANGE

While all customers flowing through the sales process will be shown all One-Click Offers regardless of whether they purchase them or not, it's possible to show specific pages to only those who said "no." I call this a Second-Chance Offer.

This is powerful because a percentage of customers will decline the One-Click Offer not because they don't see it as hugely valuable but because they thought the offer was too expensive. If the customer declines the previous opportunity to upgrade, they can be presented with a second chance to purchase in the form of a split payment plan or lower price with some elements or bonuses removed. Only customers who declined the previous offer will be taken to this page.

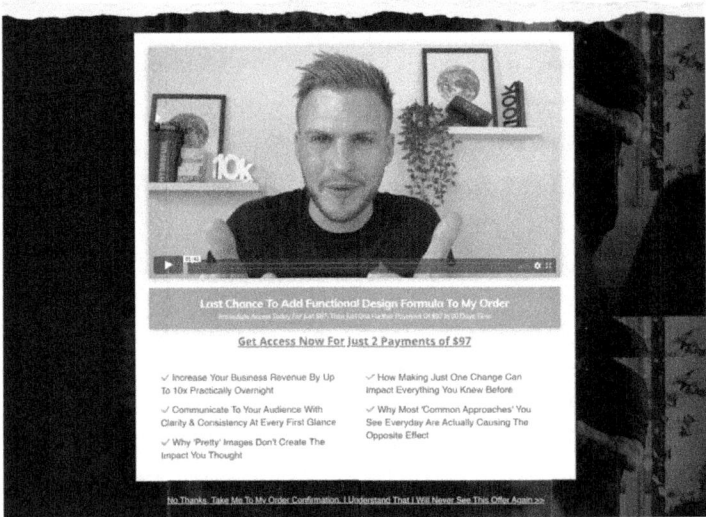

It's important here not to simply offer the same product at a cheaper price, as that erodes trust and credibility with the customer base. But by offering either a split payment plan or the slimline version of your original offer, you can make your liquidation products accessible to a larger segment of book buyers.

A Second-Chance Offer is very easy to create as it does not require any additional selling. The customer has already seen the product, so what they are getting does not need to be explained again in any great detail.

Adding this step to your funnel can allow you to increase the average cart value of every purchase without creating any new products or confusing your customers with lots of different upsells.

"I am so pleased I decided to work with Gary to market my book through a book funnel. Not only did he help me ensure that my funnel converted visitors into buyers of my book, he also advised how to best turn those readers into buyers of my higher ticket products and programmes, all while automating the entire process! I've already used this formula to sell over 1,500 books and I now have highly qualified new leads coming into my business every single day without me even lifting a finger."

Jonny Bradley—Author, Entrepreneur, Content Creator and Founder Of the SellerPro Academy

CHAPTER 9

PHASE 3: ASCEND

Now that you have successfully used your book to identify your ideal customers, you have provided greater value to those customers by offering them additional opportunities to learn from your expertise, and you have used the sale of those products to liquidate your advertising spend; it's now time to expose your book buyers to your primary desired action or core offer and continue to build that relationship with them to set them on their success path towards Oz.

This is where you switch your focus from breaking even on your advertising spend to profiting big. Depending on your specific business model and your core offering, at this stage, you may want your book buyers to:

- Complete an application.
- Request a sales call.
- Join a membership or recurring revenue stream.
- Take a free trial.
- Attend a webinar or live event.

Rather than wait and only follow up with customers hours or days later, you can take control of the sales process to bridge the gap and give those who are eager, willing and able to take the next action the ability to do so immediately.

THE BRIDGE

Marketing is all about creating bridges from what someone wants and desires to the solution that you provide.

Right now your customer has a heavy desire for reaching their Oz (as we talked about in part 1), so it's the perfect time to seed your core solution to get them there with greater convenience and in less time. This is your opportunity to ascend the relationship and help your customer understand how to take the "next step" of working with you.

Traditionally, at the end of an initial front-end sales process, a customer would be presented with a thank you page that acknowledges their purchase is complete and waves them on their way.

What is surprising about this is your "thank you" or "confirmation page" is the last page that ALL of your customers are going to see. Ever.

Think about this...

Although you can now follow up with your customers via email, direct mail and more methods we'll talk about in the next section of this book, you'll never again be in a position that 100% of your customers return to view a specific page. You'll never get 100% open rate and 100% click-through rate on an email follow up or messenger bot, and you'll never be able to reach 100% of your following in a Facebook group or by posting on Instagram.

So rather than dismissing this page as the end of the process, this is THE opportunity to make it count.

The Book Funnel Formula takes the concept of the "thank you page" and turns it on its head. Rather than being the last step in the process, it becomes the very beginning of the relationship between you and your new customer. They are crossing the bridge into your kingdom having already shown interest in you. And this is your opportunity to "woo" them and welcome them with open arms.

While you still absolutely should use this page to thank them for ordering their book and set clear expectations for delivery whether that be physical or digital access, it's important to take this moment to (at the very least) seed the idea of your next thing. Of course, not everyone is going to buy here, but it will become the initial introduction to your core offer.

The design, layout and call-to-action of this page will differ based on your business model and how you help your customers gain a result, so take a moment to review the different conversion events below, and decide which works best for you.

Breakthrough Call/Strategy Call

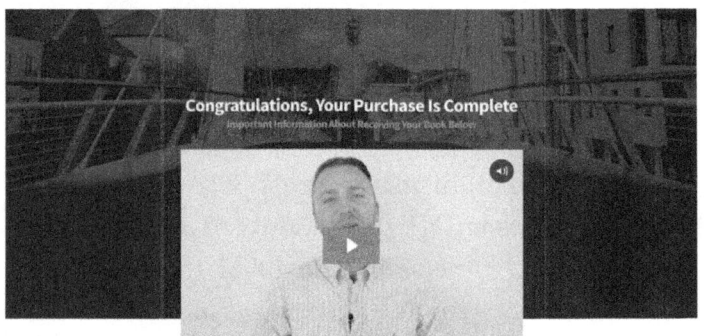

It can be difficult to sell super-expensive high-ticket products and services like coaching, consulting, masterminds or done-for-you services online, as most people are unlikely to pull out their credit card without speaking to someone first.

If you sell a high-ticket offer like this, then this is a great opportunity to change the selling environment by getting your customers on the phone to speak with you or a salesperson on your team. You then have the benefit of live feedback and can overcome objections on the fly.

On the previous page you can see how we used this format with my client, Jordan Platten, to thank the customer for their purchase and then encourage them to schedule a call with a member of his team to determine how they can help them reach their goals faster.

Free Gift/Survey

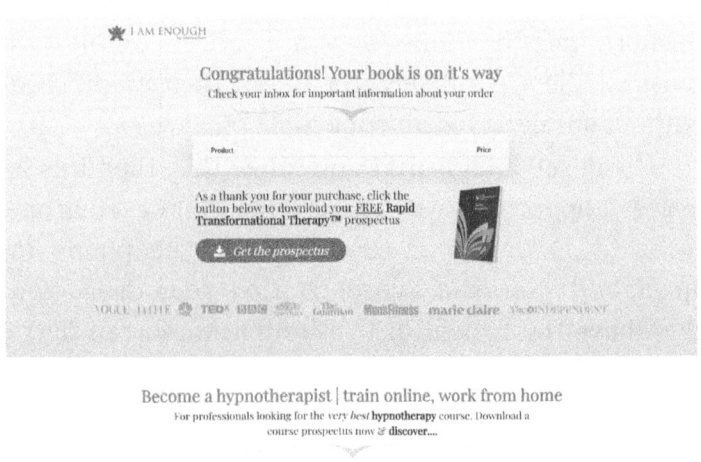

Rather than speaking to everyone at this stage, your goal may be to filter and segment customers further to determine who is super engaged and find out more about them prior to initiating a future sales conversation.

You can incentivize book buyers to provide additional information about them and their situation in a very non-salesy way by offering a free gift in return for additional information. This could be performed as a survey with multiple-choice or open-ended questions or could even be an incentive for adding your customers to a chatbot so you obtain an additional direct communication channel for future marketing and sales opportunities.

On the previous page you can see how we used this format with my client, Marisa Peer, by offering a free prospectus as an exclusive bonus for book buyers. This prospectus educates her audience about her additional products and services while allowing her to capture additional customer data.

Webinar Registration

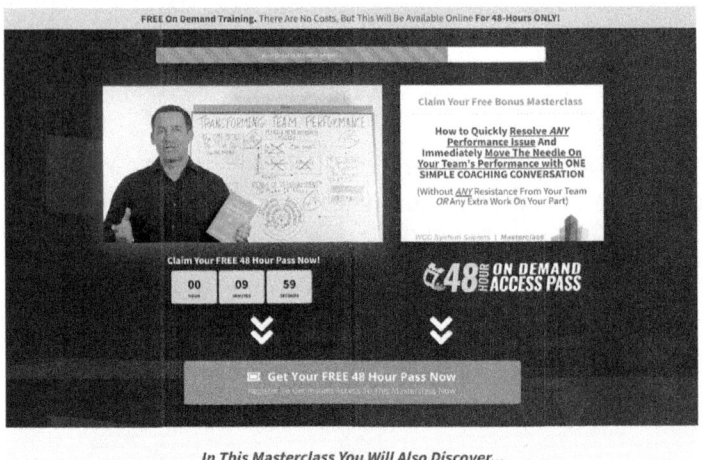

If your core offer requires additional explanation, then it makes sense to ascend your customers via a presentation. This can be delivered in the form of a webinar, training or masterclass.

You can use your thank you page to ask your customer to register for your live masterclass or set up what is known as an automated webinar where your presentation is recorded and the customer can choose a date/time to watch at their convenience.

Of course, if they don't take action to register straight away, you will still be able to follow up with them later as you have a direct communication channel with them.

On the previous page you can see how we used this format with my client, Brian Souza, by inviting his book buyers to register for his Masterclass right on his thank you page. Brian creates both urgency and a sense of convenience for his customers by offering a 48-hour on-demand access pass to his presentation. This allows the customer to consume the presentation at a time that is suitable for them but also encourages them to consume it before the 48-hour time limit expires.

Thank You Page Webinar

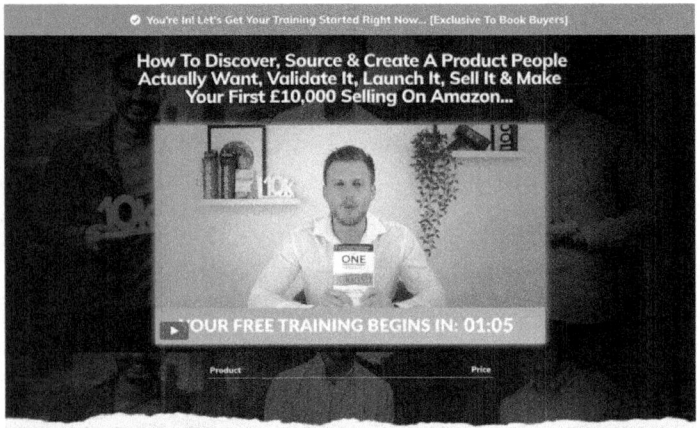

While the webinar registration relies on your new customer showing enough interest to register for the webinar and then actually show up to attend the presentation, the concept of the thank you page webinar deliberately removes all potential barriers by offering the presentation directly on the thank you page itself, providing a greater opportunity to get maximum eyeballs on your presentation.

I learned this process again from my friend and mentor, Dean Holland, who explains that by framing the presentation not as a bonus (which feels like an additional disconnected add-on) but as part of their current purchase the customer has already made, psychologically they are more likely to pay attention because if you feel like you have already paid for something, it's natural human instinct to want to get the most out of it.

On the previous page you can see how we used this format with my client, Jonny Bradley, to perform a shortened version of his webinar directly on the thank you page. Notice the language he is using is very specific. Rather than saying, "Thank you for purchasing. I now have this additional bonus thing I'd like you to watch," instead, he says, "You're in! Let's get your training started right now," framing it as something that is part of the process the customer is still going through rather than starting something new which is not part of what they already paid for. This is a subtle psychological tweak but is hugely powerful.

Offer Wall

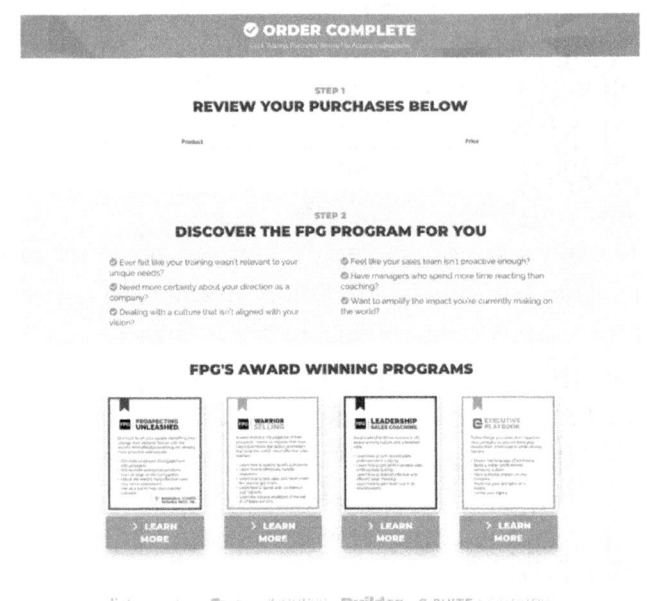

If you don't yet have a webinar presentation or a sales team to take phone calls, you can still take advantage of your "thank you page" to ascend your customers into your additional products and services using an Offer Wall.

An Offer Wall is exactly as it suggests, a wall of different offers that you have within your business. This could be links to your additional programs, other books you have written or even affiliate links to your recommended products or services which you can earn a commission on. This allows your hyperactive buyers to keep on buying for as long as they would like.

Simply by providing your customers with the opportunity to purchase something else on this page, you increase the lifetime value of your customer, putting you ahead of 99% of your competition.

On the previous page you can see how we used this format with my client, Jason Forrest, who had multiple different programs that may be suitable for his customers, depending on their goals and current situation. He invites his customer to learn more about each of the programs and allows them to choose which direction they want to take.

You shouldn't expect everyone to take action on these pages, but the magic comes from identifying the ones who do.

For those that do not take action, over the next few days, weeks, months and years, you will have follow-up systems in place to ascend each and every book buyer towards your core offerings as well as recommend suitable products and services from joint venture partners, affiliate relationships and more, consistently increasing the lifetime value of each book buyer.

Enter... the Monetization Loop.

MONETIZATION LOOP

Congratulations! By implementing the first 6 steps of *The Book Funnel Formula*, you now have a machine that creates the most powerful asset in marketing: a customer list.

Every new customer that purchases your book shares two important characteristics:

1. They have raised their hand and shown a specific interest in what you do.
2. They have shown that they are willing and able to pull out their credit card and pay for your help.

A buyer is more valuable than a new follower on Facebook, Instagram or YouTube. It's more valuable than a new member of any Facebook group. It's more valuable than any social network.

Because once established, your customer list or database of buyers is YOUR asset, and no one can take it away from you. You could build a huge following on YouTube and get your account shut down overnight with no warning; it's happened many times before. Facebook could adjust their terms to further limit reach to your followers. But your buyer's list is your data, and if you were to get closed down on one CRM or marketing automation platform, you can just download your list and take it to the next.

Unlike when selling through third parties, you now have a direct line of communication with your readers, and you can see exactly what they have previously purchased.

So how do you stay in contact with them?

You can now use marketing automation to provide further value and build a deeper relationship with your book readers by inviting them to consume additional content and sales materials in the form of webinars, video sales letters, Q&A calls and more.

The process will help you identify your dream customers who are willing and able to work with you on high-ticket projects and help you remain front and center in their minds.

Your marketing automation software has the ability to "tag" each customer based on their characteristics as well as (a feature few know even exists) score your contacts based on their behavior. So with *The Book Funnel Formula*, if a customer purchases your book, they will be tagged appropriately. And if they then go on to upgrade to a One-Click Offer, they will be tagged again and assigned points towards their lead score, based on that activity. The more engaged the customer is with your interactions, the more points will be assigned. This method allows you to rank your customer list by most engaged, and therefore, most likely to make their next purchase from you.

What would that do for your business if you knew which customers out of hundreds or even thousands on your list were most likely to be next to pull the trigger and do future business with you?

This advanced level of segmentation is only possible because you are in control of the entire sales process. You sit back and watch like a god.

So why do I call this the Monetization Loop?

By owning the customer data, you can now loop back to any stage of the sales process, encouraging your leads and customers to ascend further up your yellow brick road, further monetizing your offerings and increasing the lifetime value of every customer (LTV).

You can use this method to naturally monetize your own core offers, like modulated courses, coaching, consulting, membership communities and masterminds or put other businesses in front of your new audience in the form of joint venture partnerships where you receive a commission or profit split on each product sold to your audience.

Rather than going out and creating additional offers yourself, by owning the data, you can go out there and see who has complementary products and services that you could plug into the backend of your business to assist your customers further on the journey.

If at some stage you can no longer provide the next logical step in the customer's journey, use the Monetization Loop to integrate someone who can. They'll almost certainly be prepared to compensate you for the referral. And once you set up the deal, you can have it automatically sent to each new customer that joins your list, paying you over and over again. This is known as integration marketing.

It's even possible to get paid on the backend to recommend other people's products without establishing your own deals. Almost every industry has affiliate promotions already set up that you can promote to your list in return for a commission on each sale. Is there a software tool or additional service that's already out there that your customer would benefit from using to get closer to their Oz? Check to see if they have an affiliate plan, and add your affiliate link to your follow-up so you naturally begin to generate passive income through multiple revenue streams with little additional work.

While this type of marketing is primarily achieved through email, *The Book Funnel Formula* allows you to collect multiple data points so your Monetization Loop has the ability to spread far further than just email marketing. You can ascend your customers through email, retargeting, FB messenger, by phone, direct mail, text message or even within the actual consumption of your liquidation products.

You have the ability to quickly become omnipresent in your reader's mind, which amplifies your perceived credibility, having your customer think of you as the celebrity of your industry, when in reality, you are taking a very specific, segmented marketing approach. Let's break down some of the methods to implement this.

Email Marketing

While some may think "email marketing is dead," it's likely their experience comes from having a list of tire-kicking subscribers who originally opted in for a shiny "freebie" and had no intention of engaging or purchasing anything, ever.

The exciting thing about *The Book Funnel Formula* is that you are mailing to those who are already customers, and when people pay, they pay attention. Check out the stats below on an email follow-up campaign sent to 3,000 book buyers:

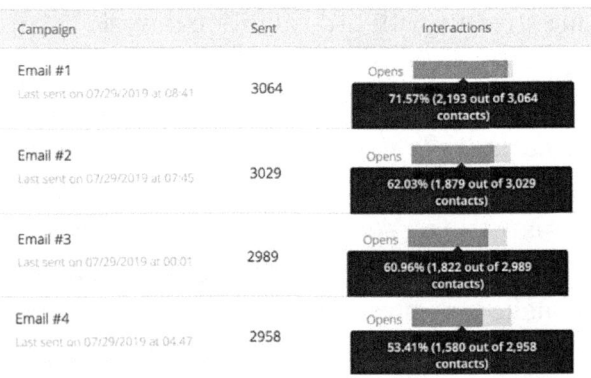

If you don't have a background understanding of email marketing, a 20% open rate would normally be considered very good.

These unheard-of open-and-click-through rates are achieved because after making a purchase, people are in a heightened sense of alert while they ensure they don't miss out on anything they already paid for. You can utilize this opportunity to show them how you can best serve them at a higher level. Remember, the key ingredient to selling anything online is getting eyeballs on what you have to offer, and you can now send those eyeballs anywhere you like, with no additional marketing cost.

Retargeting

Have you ever been to a website and then over the next couple of days or even weeks it seems like they are everywhere, following you around the internet? That's retargeting, and it's one of the most powerful ways to have someone ascend from purchasing a book to purchasing your core offerings.

While you may think of retargeting ads on Facebook or YouTube, there are also multiple ad networks that let you display your retargeting ads on other people's websites for very little cost. This includes very well-known news sites and well-respected publications.

What could it do for your perceived credibility if when your customer viewed an article on CNN or Forbes, they see your face, over and over again? By targeting your existing customers only, you can achieve celebrity-like status with very little advertising spend. How do you think your next sales call would go if the prospect had just seen your face on a globally recognized publication? Not only are they more likely to buy but they're also more likely to happily pay a premium for your services.

Messenger

Back in 2011, Facebook released its Messenger platform, which for many has replaced email as their primary method of online communication. You can utilize the Messenger platform to diversify your communication channels with your customer. A customer who tends not to open emails may well be more inclined to open a Facebook message and vice-versa.

Once someone has purchased your book, you can offer them an additional incentive which they can get for free when they join your Messenger list. Once on your list, you can use "messenger bots" to automate the interactions with your customers, allowing you to provide further value completely hands-free. While Messenger traditionally provides very high message open-rates, marketing in this way can be perceived as more intrusive than email, so it's important not to overdo it.

One aspect that we have seen particular success with is using Messenger to send reminder messages for an upcoming webinar or live event. Adding this communication channel has the ability to dramatically increase your show-up rates, once again resulting in more eyeballs on what you have to offer.

Phone

While it can be very difficult to get leads to enter real phone numbers into online webforms for fear of being bombarded by telemarketers, by asking for a phone number at the time of book purchase, this data is provided as a means of contact if any issues arise or any additional information about the order is required, thus resulting in a huge increase in genuine submissions.

This provides you or your team the opportunity to follow up with your readers to check that they received their book and strike up the conversation to find out more about them and their current situation. Very few people take this approach, and by speaking to a "real" person rather than a faceless business, it becomes more likely your customer will choose to work with you in the future over your competitors.

Direct Mail

While all of us are likely exposed to dozens of ads and hundreds of emails each and every day, how many pieces of physical mail do you receive? Likely, not many!

While direct mail used to be the primary method of advertising, it has become somewhat forgotten in the new online world, which now more than ever makes it an excellent opportunity to stand out to your customers.

If you are shipping out physical books, then you will naturally already be mailing to the customers' physical address. Why not include an insert card telling them about your additional offers?

Like I mentioned previously in this book, there's something magical about the future relationship with a customer who actually has a physical copy of your book at their home or in their office, and the same goes for any future mailings. When performed correctly, sending your customers tangible, personalized promotional materials in the mail builds trust, credibility and relationship like almost nothing else.

Text Message

Just like with email and Messenger, there are platforms that allow you to send automated text message broadcasts to your customers. While I tend to prefer this method for customer-service-based operations like book delivery notifications, this communication method can also be used for future marketing efforts.

By opening the conversation with a customer service announcement like a shipping notification or delivery confirmation, any future marketing communications via text message tend to feel less invasive, and therefore, your customers will be more responsive. I recommend, however, that you keep the frequency low so as not to bombard your customers with unwanted messages and risk tainting the relationship.

Product Consumption

This is one of my favorite methods of customer ascension and one you should already be thinking about if you have designed your liquidator products correctly from the previous section of this book.

The job of your liquidator products is not only to educate and solve the problems of your customers but also to prime them for your next thing. With that in mind, you want to make it as seamless as possible for your customers to ascend from one product to the next. A lot of people don't buy simply because they are not sure what they need or what is right for them. By laying out the success path in front of them, you can make it very simple for them to know what they should consume next and how they access it.

As you can see from the example below, rather than the customer completing their training inside the member's area and leaving, we provide the next steps right there as part of the product. This is particularly powerful because your sales messages are framed as additional content, which increases the overall consumption and likelihood of ascension.

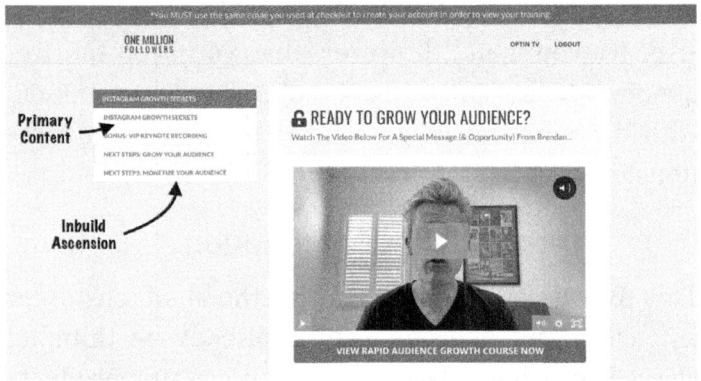

I hope that by revealing the multitude of possibilities the Monetization Loop provides, I have inspired you to think about monetizing your book in ways you may never even have considered. And while the possibilities are endless, it's important to start small and not get overwhelmed. I recommend you get started promoting 1 or 2 backend offers through 1 or 2 communication channels and continue building your empire from there.

Do you have a product or a service that you think would integrate seamlessly into my business to help my readers and loyal customers? I'm always on the lookout for future joint venture partners. Reach out and let me know at: jv@garywhite.com.

PART 3

MAKING IT HAPPEN!

"When I first spoke with Gary he put me at ease instantly. He aligned with my vision and my ethos, and I trusted him immediately. I just knew that this is somebody I want to work with to grow my business. Launching my book funnel changed my business massively by giving me a new and sustainable way to attract new leads and customers. We generated $20,000 in revenue on launch week alone and the funnel has since become a 5-figure monthly earner. I am so envious right now of everyone lucky enough to read this book. Gary is handing you the strategies that I've paid him literally thousands of dollars to learn and implement! If you are launching a book to start or grow your business this is a must read for sure!"

**Jordan Platten—Author, Speaker
and Founder of Affluent.co**

CHAPTER 10

HOW I HELP PEOPLE JUST LIKE YOU

I hope by now you're excited about the possibilities of taking back control of the book sales process and feel motivated to take action and get started creating your own book funnel that fuels your business with your ideal clients and customers.

If you're still not sure if a book funnel is right for you, I want you to consider just how valuable it would be to have a direct communication channel with everyone that reads your book. If you had the ability to speak to every single reader directly without being at the mercy of any corporations or global tech companies, do you think you could land just one new consulting client? Do you think you could change just one person's life by offering to go deeper with them?

And if there's 1, there are probably 10 or 50 or 100, or 1,000+. They're already out there, and by using the methods in this book, you can find them, help them and reap the financial rewards of doing so for years to come.

The bigger question is what is your time worth, and does it make sense for you to try and figure this out on your own and do it alone? Or do you make the decision to work with an experienced marketing funnel expert who specializes in implementing the formula and has the ability to eradicate the tech roadblocks that so often put people off establishing any form of automated online systems in the first place?

The fact of the matter is you have a couple of options right now.

You can simply shelve this idea "for later."

You can start investigating the process of piecing together the different steps required to build a successful book funnel on your own. Be aware that this approach requires that you take the time to learn many different skill sets and wear many different hats, from copywriting to design to email marketing to fulfillment setup, offer creation and beyond.

You could hire out those tasks to freelancers who each have experience in their individual area and hope that you can bring them all together in a cohesive way.

Or you could work directly with an experienced marketing funnel expert like me, with a proven process and specific sequence of direct-action steps which when completed correctly, consistently result in book funnel campaigns that have the ability to fuel your business for not just months but also years to come.

When you work with me to transform your book into an automated online sales machine that pays you time after time on autopilot, you get my years of experience making sure you avoid the common pitfalls and don't trip, stumble or unnecessarily drag your feet.

The reality is, it's taken me more than 5 years to get to this point, with hundreds of tests, failures and surprise outcomes which puts me in a unique position to fast-track that process for you into about 30 days or less. There's truly nothing I enjoy more than working with influential leaders and entrepreneurs whose passion runs so deep they literally wrote the book on their subject. That means I'd love to work with you.

Rest assured, when we work together, you get the personalized opportunity to get your entire book funnel done right and done fast. We will have scheduled phone calls, and you will have direct access to me as I guide you step by step through the process, all while my team builds the whole thing out for you from scratch.

Before you know it, you'll have transformed your book into a fully automated sales and marketing machine that actively raises the hands of your ideal readers and identifies your dream clients and customers, regardless of your business model, technical ability or previous experience in selling online.

CHAPTER 11

THE NEXT STEP

If you have arrived on this page after reading this entire book, then thank you and congratulations. I can't wait to see you implement *The Book Funnel Formula*.

Now this is where the average person stops. The average person reads a book, gets inspired but ultimately takes no action.

Simply by making it to the very end of this book tells me you're not average. You have a message to share with the world, and I'm passionate about helping you do that.

I hope you now feel motivated to take action and get started transforming your book into a completely automated sales machine that fuels your business with your dream clients and customers using *The Book Funnel Formula*.

As you now know, by implementing the methods outlined in this book, you can deliver a much higher-quality customer experience to your readers while profitably growing your own customer database so you have the ability to rapidly scale your marketing, exposure and reach to levels you previously may not have thought possible.

Now I'd love to hear from you.

As I said, there's truly nothing I enjoy more than working with influential leaders and entrepreneurs whose passion runs so deep they literally wrote the book on the subject.

If that's you and you'd like to further explore how my team and I can help you implement *The Book Funnel Formula* for yourself, then I invite you to take the next step and complete a Book Funnel Idea survey.

This short survey will help me understand what you do, what your goals are and if a book funnel is right for you. It takes no more than five minutes to complete, and of course, I keep all of your information completely confidential. To get started, visit:

TheBookfFunnelFormula.com/apply

Once your survey is submitted, I will be notified and will review it personally. If I think there's a good fit and we can genuinely help you, my team will reach out to schedule a call.

This call is all about helping you decide if working together to create your own high-converting book funnel is a good fit for both of us. Unfortunately, we're not able to work with everyone, so this is not a sales call. It's more of a two-way interview to make sure we agree this is a good match.

We'll ask you some questions, and you can ask as many questions as you like. Then we can take it from there. There's no obligation on your part until you have decided to become a client.

Sound good?

Ok, it's time to close this book and take massive action on making it happen.

I look forward to hearing from you, and more importantly, working together to transform the way you are currently using your book to grow your business.

To your continued success and to getting your book into the hands of your dream customers.

Gary White

"When Gary came through one of my mentoring programs I could see there was something different about him. Not only did he already have a brilliant marketing mind but he was a serial action taker (Something that is lacking in a lot of 'entrepreneurs'). I've since seen him go from strength to strength and I would definitely be going to him if we ever need help with a F+O offer. He is someone who understands the mechanics of creating a high converting funnel that says and does the right things to turn strangers to customers."

Jon Penberthy—7 Figure Marketer, Entrepreneur, International Trainer and Founder of AdClients.com

ABOUT GARY WHITE

Gary is a marketing funnel expert, author, consultant and coach for influential leaders, entrepreneurs and business owners looking to thrive in the online marketplace. Considered a #1 authority on engineering high-converting sales funnels, Gary is the funnel expert other experts go to when they need help with their own sales funnels.

As one of the Top 30 ClickFunnels™ designers, Gary was awarded #1 funnel design by Russell Brunson at the ClickFunnels Design-A-Thon event in Boise, ID. He has worked directly with Russell and the ClickFunnels team to design and create many of the in-app templates currently installed within the ClickFunnels platform and utilized by thousands of members daily.

With clients all around the globe, Gary has built funnels for some of the biggest names in the marketing world, including many recipients of the prestigious ClickFunnels "2 Comma Club Award" (issued for generating over $1 million through single sales funnel) and is now on a mission to revolutionize the way nonfiction books are purchased online.

Gary lives, works and travels the world with his amazing partner, Sammi. Sammi is the invisible driving force between everything Gary does to serve clients, including end-to-end funnel design and development.

To learn more about Gary, visit:

GaryWhite.com

KEY RESOURCES

While I did not want to confuse and overcomplicate the flow of this book by mentioning each and every tool and resource I use to implement *The Book Funnel Formula*, I have, instead, gone ahead and created a full list of my recommended tools and resources for you at:

TheBookFunnelFormula.com/resources

GARY WHITE

NOTES

THE BOOK FUNNEL FORMULA

READER BONUS!

Want to see behind the scenes of how to design, build & launch your own high-converting book funnel? I've put together a special recording, previously reserved only for my private book funnel clients that deep dives into the entire Book Funnel Formula process and literally hands you the easy button to have all of this up and running in a matter of days.

If I'm still doing this by the time you are reading this book, then head straight over to your computer and watch the video now. It's absolutely free.

WATCH TODAY!

TheBookFunnelFormula.com/secret